T0037517

JOY *is the* JUSTICE
We GIVE OURSELVES

J. DREW LANHAM

HUB CITY PRESS
SPARTANBURG, SC

Editor: John Lane
Cover Design: Meg Reid
Cover illustration: Tristan Kromopawiro

Library of Congress
Cataloging-in-Publication Data

Names: Lanham, J. Drew (Joseph Drew), author.
Title: Joy is the justice we give ourselves
  J. Drew Lanham.
Description: Spartanburg, SC: Hub City Press
Berkeley, CA: Distributed to the trade by
Publishers Group West, 2024.
Identifiers:
  LCCN 2023051730 (print)
  LCCN 2023051731 (ebook)
  ISBN 9798885740302 (hardback)
  ISBN 9798885740340 (epub)
Subjects:
  LCSH: Nature—Poetry.
  LCGFT: Nature poetry. | Essays.
Classification:
LCC PS3612.A58536 J69 2024 (print)
LCC PS3612.A58536 (ebook)
DDC 811/.6—dc23/eng/20231108

LC record available at https://lccn.loc.gov/2023051730

"Joy is the Justice We Give Ourselves" appeared in *Emergence*; "Wish Thrush" appeared in *Orion*; "With
Wilderness, Liberty, and Justice for All" appeared in *Sierra*; "Nine New Revelations for the Black Bird-Watcher"
appeared in Vanity Fair; "How We Spend Our Days" appeared on the *How We Spend Our Days* site;
"Dead is the New Black" appeared in *USA Today*; "Nativist Namaste" appeared in New Suns; "Coffee Black"
appeared in 12 Mile Review; "Winter Kill" appeared on the Great Northern Festival website.

Manufactured in the United States of America
First Edition

HUB CITY PRESS
200 Ezell Street
Spartanburg, SC 29306
864.577.9349 | www.hubcity.org

This Joy I have, the world didn't give it to me!
This joy, I have, the world didn't give it to me!
This joy, I have, the world didn't give it to me!
So the world can't take it! The world can't take it!
The world can't take it away!

—SHIRLEY CAESAR

Table of Contents

Foreword

These poems and pieces of prose are a manifestation of an old spiritual my grandmother Mamatha used to sing when I was a child. It was her own declaration of life, liberty, and a pursuit of happiness otherwise denied by an American society rife with racism, misogyny, and all manner of injustices. She'd lived through Jim Crow, two world wars, a Great Depression, several recessions, two "police actions" (Korea and Vietnam), assassinations of Medgar Evers, Martin Luther King Jr., Malcom X, John F. and Robert F. Kennedy, church bombings, cross burnings, protests, civil unrest, uncivil struggle, a woman refusing to sit in the rear, a civil rights movement, a World War I combat-veteran husband whose scarred lungs still burned from mustard gas, a moonshot, and an only son who died a decade before she did. Nine decades of unimaginable change, and yet she somehow still found joy.

Now in this Anthropocene, an epoch I prefer to call the *Identocene*, we all seek our who-ness in the midst of change that operates at several orders of magnitude beyond Mamatha's wildest imagining. So much has changed but then not so much. There are still wars and rumors of them. There is unrest and upheaval. There is racism and every other kind of bias exerted by social media megaphone. Schools have become killing fields and a president promoted revolution. People die by the police because their Black lives don't matter.

So from whence does my joy come? Can I sing her joy song? Yes, I can! I'm not religious like my grandmother and I cruise from atheist to Zen several times an hour. But there were lessons in her resilience. Nature is my goddess and birds, the heavenly hosts. Miracles occur by evolutionary adaptation and seasonal migration. Between equinoxes and solstices, on the edges of sunrise and sunset, I discover my best self. Wherever I can stand in wild witness, watch surf come and go and sanderlings play tag within that surging, I can sometimes defer the troubles of the world to have hope in something better. As injustice and inhumanity rule so much, I think some on problems, but feel more on possibility. That's where the joy comes in and I hold tightly to it. I write to the things I see, smell, feel, and hear. My heartbeat sets the rhythm to thrush song. So much within this book comes from those moments that can take trouble and, for a bit, transform it into some kind of happiness that keeps me going. Be advised, every poem isn't an ode to joy, and yes, sometimes there is sadness, or anger within the words. It is the life I lead, the Black skin I'm happily in, the love I try to give. But it's my hope that the feel of the work herein helps the reader know that wildness is at the center of my joy. The tame world didn't give it to me. And I won't let that world take it away.

J. Drew Lanham, Summer 2023

TO NOTICE

Don't be surprised that I have suddenly
taken to the woods. I hate routine.

ZORA NEALE HURSTON

At Altitude

From up here
I sometimes look down
on this land we sometimes call home
collectively (sometimes),
that some called home long ago,
but now
I cannot see the color of a single human soul.
It is impossible to know who loves whom,
whether bread is being broken at tables,
what stress or strife fractures home and hearth
what binds in kindness or care,
whether life lingers sweet, or death drops bitter quick—
I cannot know any of this from up here.
Only how shades of brown, tinges of gray,
stretches of green fingering
wet crotches where water might be,
pull me into it
so deep I can hardly breathe.

For brief moments at velocity, chasing speed of sound,
all stands still for a second or two
in the frame of plexiglass to which I am assigned:
seat 8A, Business Class.
I cannot see any manner of *Homo sapiens* identity
or presence ever wrought, for an instant
everything is nothing and it is all overwhelming
wild vastness I desire to swallow me,
whole soul—
devour my nothing into its nothingness.

I see from nearly forty thousand feet high what
earth pushed up
has been worn down by sun wind snow ice fire and rain,
rendered as art in relief.
All of it is time. Time.
Time ticking by in grains of soil once solid stone
where none could witness until time made it clear what was.
Time now wearing apart in what no one could ever count
underneath clouds no one could ever possess.
It is in these moments flying higher than any hawk might imagine,
an obsession of mountains, prairie, splines of rivers.
Basins flattened fanned out,
backbones of ridges flanked by bared ribs of rock
left behind from countless ages of time and physics
having their way with one another.
Time tumbles the physics rough.
Both consent.

And then the moment passes.
Center pivot circles appear as targets for desire.
We want what we want.
Have to make
wild nothing into our something.
Progress, some might say.
Humanity marks the vast with fence lines,
sections that can be owned or commanded
by tractor, plow, center pivot, or black angus.

The geometry fucks geology.
Did not ask for what it took by force.
There is discord everywhere.
Politics rapes peace.
I cannot see the hate at altitude,
but feel it inside.
I remember.
Glass and steel catches light to glint it back as reminder.

I remember.

Here I am up here sucking gas, carbonizing.
Making my own outsized tracks.
There we are down there sod busting, planting,
paving, grazing, drilling, draining.

Being us undeniably together in the whole mess.

I find comfort more in past tense of what I saw
three hundred miles back before
my past-tense brain caught up
with my now heart.

Wheels down and more school children are dead.

Denial was for a while
a wild place on the map
down there.

Big Easy Black Bird

There are stories
the string of beads would tell,
hanging now as they do
from the sweep of live oak branch,
festooned like so much glamped-up Spanish moss.
What manner of drunken debauch warranted arboreal launch?
What was bared? What stayed hidden?
Who sinned? Was everyone the next day forgiven?
Does God, on that day, sneak a sip?
Would Jesus throw baubles at Mary Magdalene?
Ask her for a glimpse?

A crow strolls by,
black as night beneath a golden strand,
hanging a bit more than head high,
wobbling a bit in its corvid walk.
Drunk? I wonder.
Hungover under the overhanging glimmer,
it is the privilege of voyeur bird
to see. But not tell.

Wonder with my morning bourbon,
at my lips to hide the smile growing,
what kind of Big Easy crow
I would have been.

The Sweetest War

For every sugary sweet sip, for each nectary nip, there's a ruby-throated war being waged. Whether blue sage blossom or sugar-filled bottle, aerial combat appears more urgent than cordiality, defense more critical than dining. Twittering and buzzing by at breakneck speed, any energy earned is immediately frittered away on fast and furious fights. The ground gained is measured in calories. Low-level chases that barely pass above the Bermuda grass escalate into cloudward pursuits. A momentary hover is a feathered gauntlet thrown down. Dares cannot be denied. Loyalties lie in some other dimension—perhaps beyond hummingbird-knowing, there is the blossom. There is the bottle. Every fast-flying feathered thing is a foe. The victories last mere seconds. And the peace passes in half the time.

Throughout it all there are no guns aimed and no shots fired. No murders. No necks knelt upon. No raging fires or looting. There are no presumptions of innocence or guilt. There's no racism. It is existence boiled down to feathers and flight. It is nature-survival on a broken piedmont backyard scale. There is this story to report—and I am the wondering and grateful eye-witness watching it all.

Dead is the New Black

Sitting here
three days removed from what some call Independence Day
The Fourth of July
Bound by anger
Chained and confused by fear
'Merica they told me
was becoming a better place
Equality, pursuit of happiness
Life liberty
Shit like that
Barack's in the Oval Office
Shouldn't that suffice?
But today after another two of us were shot down
like rabid dogs in the street
I'm hearing anything
but some cracked bell's toll
Feeling doubtful of the word "free"
I'm an endangered species without cause for protection or concern
My life doesn't matter
to those behind the badges
The ones who lifted their hands
Swore to some lie called an oath
to serve and protect
—as my Daddy used to say, *Funny but not laughable.*
Seems the laws and rules put in place
Ain't nothing but a license to roam
Intimidate
Harass and abuse.

Black and bruised
seems the acceptable daily news

Yep. There'll be an investigation though
to determine what took place.
Meanwhile
two more Black men
died at the man's hands
And the horror streams
like a commercialized nightmare on CNN.

Today I'm feeling anything but free
Nothing like a human deserving liberty
Maybe I should just stay at home
Don't drive my car or expect fair shake
Sh*t—maybe I'll just give up now
"Make America great again!"
Isn't that what the people who wanna be in charge say?

Fuck—now I gotta have that talk with my son once again—
"Bow down, Colby—don't look Massuh Officer in the eye
I love you and want you to come home son—*just be a good Negro*
I don't want you to die."

By the stat count
dark skinned men
are on the way down
Thank your local yokel for the service

Besides us being Goddamned niggers—
it seems any murder is justifiable
long as there's a taillight out

So, I'll tell my son the news—
wait with dread whenever he's out
until he's locked down somewhere
safe—
and alive
I'll worry and suffer in doubt

Beyond being the next sad sorry
the next day's repeated headline
My head's in a sad place
Not on birds or wildness
Or wandering
It's come down to a matter
of simplest human survival
I'm wondering
what's keeping ME
or my kin
from being the next sad story
The next among hundreds
Lying there lifeless
Breathless and bloody
because of my brown skin

Somehow, someway we all
deserve better

I want to believe it will someday come
But for now
Today
It's just a dream turned nightmare

But until further notice—

Dead is the new Black, y'all
Race is a lethal condition
Being a man of color
That's the national sin.

Just Being

To many in these times, the hours fall by as joyless days. We worry and fret over everything. I feel in some ways as if I'm in a minefield, not knowing what next step might explode underneath me. Each word is a transgression, every thought a crime waiting to be committed. I try my hardest to be my best but I know at some point soon I will fail. Isn't it inevitable? What if in my earnest attempts to be human, my imperfections somehow mar the perfect person I never was? Who will report my wrongs and send me to ruin? Will I show up here or on the six o'clock news? We are overwrought and wrung out with angst waiting for the worst to happen because we'll be better off in some other end. It all has my head hurting and my heart sore.

Is there some cure?

Hate has found its way into my daily think-stream for people I don't even know, beyond what they tweet or what the headlines tell me to believe. I cannot find the wherewithal to dam the flow and make it stop. Perhaps if I could only learn to somehow ignore but then I cannot deny or turn a blind eye to so much going wrong. There are far too many *ists* and *isms* still here. Fighting them all at once is like an eternal career in uphill stone rolling. Just call me Sisyphus Jr. The stress keeps me up late into the night and makes me want to lapse into sleep midday, numbing even more. Withdrawing seems the easy answer—just closest family and a few treasured friends—and always wildness and birds. Wildness. And Birds.

I guess tomorrow (which has just become *now*) is another day.

But in the midst of all this Anthropocene angst, I'm an ecologist, tending to an earth that continues to spin, in spite of all the countering effects of the schisms and the *isms*. The conservationist working to hold on to what's left and the cultural ornithologist bent to thinking about the bird sense of humanity. It means I must necessarily work, as Aldo Leopold wrote, "in a world of wounds." For all of the things to worry over in the sociopolitically hot news stream, the state of nature is extinctions.

I'll be okay. If I just read the right books and watch the right things. Somewhere, some thought police will allow me clearance. And the birds will accept me if my flaws don't impede their free flight. I seek distracted focus through them when I can. But an alternate life insists on interceding. Responsibility and expectation. Discipline or procrastination.

I cannot put everything off forever. But I try. And then the night falls and escape by intermittent napping finally calls. I'll wake soon from way too little R.E.M. to *w-r-e-n* chatter and roll the rock upslope again. I'll just think of it as job security. Keeping myself out of the sandy hole that fills back double with each shovel of worry thrown out has become the work. Sanity slips into unremarkable dreams in the witching hour. I toss and turn, then finally up with first bird's song. Cardinal and aforementioned wren take turns from day-to-day on songster prima. It is in this quiet time, I steal away alone—with even the cat still asleep in feline somnambulance—to the yoga mat and the growing chorus outside. For those moments in whatever pose my aging body half bends, I am grateful for peace that will end when the rest of my world awakens. Then, as every responsible person puts head down to grindstone and work, carrying forward some responsible discipline, I'll steal away out there, where joy comes in the form of feathers and I can be a movement of one before the hamster wheel spins—hashtagged to a singular cause: just being.

Come Autumn

The calendar says fall. The sun says summer is done—an equinox has come. Still, the heat climbs to make me think of June. Confused, I turn to the wild things. They all agree—it is the season for which we have no name. Our wings have brought us here in days of lessening light. We need no pages or clocks to tell us the time. We simply know it is. The deer too know a turn is on the way. I'm anxious—feeling the edges of it at dawn and dusk, as they must. The katydids have gone quiet, letting the crickets have the night. There is no choir at dawn. The wrens sing half-hearted duets. Come cool now, autumn. We are ready.

How We Spend Our Days

This day is those days which are these days of many-hued leaves leaving. These are the days the wind comes in and rattles fall's cage, stripping the maples and poplars nude of saffron and scarlet but leaving them wrinkled, soiled clothes on beeches and oaks. These are the days of white-throated sparrows arriving in the back yard to sing of old Sam Peabody's poverty-stricken Canadian times. These are the days of deer chasing, of bucks' antler rubbing, of does' white tails lifting, of future fawn-making, the convergent intersected result. These are the days of me wishing I was watching them ghost through at dawn. Of me wishing I was waiting until dusk for them to reappear. Of me wishing I was above it all, voyeuring into wood's lust. These are the days of the beaver moon hiding behind earth's shadow. Me getting out of a warm bed at 2 a.m. to see it turn a pinker shade of pale. It is the day of me howling to myself.

This is the day that becomes the days of stress coming, expectation swelling, perfection failing. Familial ailing. Holidays. These are the days of true friend revelations. These are the days of double-dose vaxxing. Boosting. Hoping that odd coughs are just coughs. These are the days of still masking. These are the days of wondering why Black lives don't matter beyond marches or unarmed Negroes dying. These are indeed the times that try our souls—one day of despairing multiplied into too many and knowing that justice is an ephemeral thing lain at the intersection of *juris prudence* and luck of the jury drawn.

These are the days of the very last leftover katydid half-humming. These are the days of witnessing black birds gathering. Flocking. Peppering bruised purple evening sky. Feathered barometers as accurate as the meteorological coin flip. These are the days of autumn becoming winter before winter is official. These are the days of winter wrens in woodpiles chattering, not caring whether it is winter or not. These are the days of kinglets ruling over thickets with ruby and golden crowns. These are the days of first frost. Of sapsuckers mewing like arboreal cats. These are the days of cuddling a real cat. A tabby cat. A purring tabby cat that trusts my lap for a few moments of napping. This is the day I envy feline relaxation technique. This is the day to be a copycat.

These are the days when Christmas moves to the front of the hyper-capitalistic line and any other holiday gets bumped out of mind. These are days the once tender summer green gets bit by below-32 degrees and curled to crispy brown. These are the days of second and then third cup coffee-ing. These are the days of cardinals being redbirds. Juncos being snowbirds. Flickers being yellowhammers. Vultures being buzzards. These are the days of flip flops, chilly toes, and fleece vests for warming. These are the days of ashy ankles needing more lotion. This is the day I don't care about what I look like. These are the days that the mustard greens get bitter and taste best. The days of rutabaga bottoms mashed to a pulp and boiled purple top turnips with butter. These are the days of deep-fried turkeys and cornbread dressing (never ever ever *stuffing*). These are the days of sweet potato pie (punkins are for jack-o-lanterns and for fake coffee flavorings). This is not the day to visit the scale.

These are the kitty-corner days. The nearby faraway days. The days of converting celsius to fahrenheit and back. Why, because zero isn't always zero and thirty-two can be hot as hell. These are the days of ellipses and words never written but thought.

These are the days between warblers and waterfowl, between butterbutt yellow rumps in the myrtle bush and butterball buffleheads on the farm pond. These are the days of doing downward-facing dog with the non-napping cat alongside. This is the day I thought of tadpoles in puddles as commas which made me pause as a boy. Still do as a man. These are the days of goldenrod the color of sun. Of sumac red as blood. These are the mellow days of minor chord wringing tears from my head. These are the days of chipmunk hoarding scurry. These are the days of take your time, but hurry—'cause there's not enough time.

These are the days when slop fat pigs used to wonder how long it would be before the cold day came and it was the end of their time. That the sharp knife and the heavy ax and the boiling vat would come callin'. These are the days when November thinks of retiring. These are the days, all wrapped into one. This is a day in my mind. A day in the life. What date you ask? Yesterday or today. Or maybe tomorrow. I can't remember now. Each present has become yesterday way too fast. Tomorrow is today already. This day past tense to that. All of this swirls before I wake or in a dream or between yoga mat and shower and first call from someone wanting something I procrastinated doing. This is a day of another Zoom. There is something due this day, I'm pretty sure. Perhaps it is what you read now. Perhaps not. Here it is, anyway, for your perusal. This day is singularly plural. This is the day I dared write down what one day of musing might be like. The day I thought about who, what, where, and when brings peace to my life and who, what, where, and when shreds my life to pieces. This is the day of a single sigh, an extended exhale. Hoping to take in another, so as to keep the stream of consciousness flowing.

Of Wind and Wings

Feeling something in the air today. Not sure what, whether good or bad weather. There is an uncertain swirling, an inevitable coming. When there is something in the wind, the wild things know first—the wild things with wings perhaps the most. Waterfowl move willingly with the urging of storms. Torrential rain, fog thick as clabbered cream, stinging sleet and ice, wet snow—it all seems to inspire them, encourage them to harder drive them on. I wonder on those rare days when I'm fortunate enough to witness hundreds of ring-billed gulls swarming like so much garrulous snow over multitudes of ducks—blackjacks, cans, bluebills, redheads, baldpate, grey ducks, and a few green-winged teal, gathered like feathered fleas on a tiny two-acre farm pond as if it were a big brackish bay—from where these wanderers have come? What trials have they survived? What obstacles overcome? And then in watching them there, I fall into flight envy. I ponder for a moment as they take to the air, wedging to fly a tight direct line then bank and turn towards someplace maybe far away or close by, what life up there must be like.

And then as the sharp whistling of their wings cuts into my momentary dreams, I look down to my two-footed grounding. I brace my wingless humanity against the cold wet they cherish and in gratitude for the differences—smile.

By Lunar Logic

Trying to recalculate the good constants amidst the bad. Looking up sometimes helps. Cloudy overcast or star-stitched clear. Full and eclipsed. Waxing or waning. Crescent, half, or quarter. Blood, Flower, Hunter, Planting, Beaver, Wolf, Buck, Harvest, or whatever. Holding water or draining. Whether I can see you or not, you are there—in your orbit never failing—pulling my heart to you as though it were ocean tide. Soul is ebb. Love is flow. Tonight, most grateful for that. When humanity fails—and it always does—I find a solution to most sad equations in that nature does not.

Denali

And then I was the universe—
but only a speck of dust in it.
I was ruler of all I could see—
yet subject to every whim
of the expanse and willingly so.
I was everything. But nothing.
I was wings, claws, jaws and fins;
all heart and no brain.
I was beast, mountain, sky above,
tundra below.
I was river braided into itself.
I was spruce tree tall. I was wildflower
low.
                    I was ice flow.
        That is to say,
I was time itself grinding slow to silt
all in my path
then surging to leave lovely ruin behind.
Retreating into myself too.
Hot. Cold.
Full of fear but all brave.
Wise. Foolish. Crevasse. Summit.
Man. But mostly child.
Every bit free for the wanting
toenail to head.
I became wind, sun, moon, snow.
I grunted, growled, burrowed, swam, rutted, fought—
made love to the earth.

Every nerve wriggled bucked flashed
and flew up from within me as if wild—
because in that moment,
I was every thing.

Cultivating Entropy (A Mess Made)

I have cultivated a mess. Used neglect as a tool. Tame is an illusion I feed myself. Things gape and grow. They sprawl waywardly and yawn wide open their sweet-scented maws of death. They fruit. They flower. They flourish. They entice. They scramble for the light with no regard for control or limit. Some spin traps of silk to suck life from the careless into themselves. Others grasp by tendril, climb on top, wind through and around whatever they must. Some interrupt order by sprout. Some ripen and rot to live again through shit or shift in some other untended spot. They all know the days are shortening and with them, their lives. The green tires of the work, peeks around the corner to blue. Senescence will be rest. Wilt, final fate. Autumn curls her come hither finger from a few weeks away. Dormancy lurks. But not yet. It is lush and desperate. The tangling feels right, as if I could become it, or be lost in it. I feel it heavily these August days, through bare feet and beating heart, craving rootedness in this earth.

Miscellany

Bits and pieces of this and that. Most days it's hard to focus on any one thing—so I live in a blur to take it all in. Looking around to watch for what's ahead—but sneaking peeks behind. Wandering to be still. Finding certain kinds of company so I can be alone. It's a fascination with fragments; an obsession with wholly consuming obsessions. I build tiny houses of mindless brick-a-brat. It's not a deficit of attention from which I suffer—but a surplus of it that spills to fill each and every corner of my brain. Wanting to know most what I can't is job security. Introversion makes the best of friends. The dam is down and the off-switch broken to on. The overflow ends up trickling heartward. I drown in it because I choose to inhale—and not swim out to save myself.

·

Sunflowers, as if

As if—
to outshine the very sun
that birthed them; as if to out yellow
whatever yellow thought it could be;
as if to glow beyond the waning day;
as if to become irresistible to the birds
who sing as if dismayed in the sudden appearance
of so much beauty;
as if to show—
that in the midst of all the wrong
and hate
and bitter ugliness there is in this world—

they stand
as if,
there were not.

If a Butterfly

By what destructive force did the dismembering come to pass? Was it by some bird's predatory instinct in search of a meal? Or maybe it happened in a sudden hot and harsh wind—a late summer downpour come on without warning that dashed it apart, sending it screaming loud as gnat wings, beating the way lepidopteran kind do when thrown against a hardened blossom to be rendered mysteriously here, like iridescent pages ripped silently as tissue from an artist's crazed reverie. More likely it was a lizard, an anole moody green as grass that would not let the lovely flutterer pass. Or a mantis, praying for close passage and so hoping, cloaked with dagger hands lying in wait to devour the soft soul and discard the now useless wings glittering in the afternoon sun. By whatever entropic entomological god the butterfly ended and became these scattered pieces of its former floating fluttering nectar-seeking self, the beauty it was in past whole form is really no less than it is in present scattered dead-as-stone state. I know this bio-physic because I too deteriorate—daily—but not so stylishly. And now it is a puzzle—a mystery unsolvable but by wild guesses thrown like blind darts. There is no target at which to aim, only a beginning followed by certain end. We cannot reassemble life by wish or whim. Cannot always know cause or time. The patchwork of swallowtail lying flightless forever between my feet I cannot make solvent by perching on flower again, proves this point well.

We are all made to one day be dismantled things.

TO BE WILD

In short, all good things are wild and free.

HENRY DAVID THOREAU

Wish Thrush

Perhaps I'm just twisted—seeing birds in everything. Every. Thing. A break from the monotonous must-do necessaries (Why do today what can be worried over tomorrow) and forgotten summer-hoarded shells fallen out of an old bag were just the entropic entangle needed to inspire a fantasy ramble. Without much thought and minimal rearranging, a thicket-dwelling gray-winged wishwelker (*welker* being the Old Afro-Dutch for thrush) flew out! I'm not sure where one might find the species on a field guide page. Everyone from Johnny Jim Audubon to Kenn Kaufman seems to have forgotten it. From what I recall, the old folks called 'em "farther muckers," owing to their legendary long-distance intergalactic peregrinations. It didn't utter a single identifying call and I'm not so sure it even sings. I'm surmising that it was miraculously created on the first day of the week by a lesser pseudo-god, given to easy distraction, procrastination, and an admiration for adaptation and evolution as wondrously divine—and too, a keen noticer who sees migration as miraculously sublime. Guessing too that the inspiration came from some attention to nonattention and wandering thoughts. Now this is the kind of deity with whom I fall in line!

Regardless of origin, it is immediately listable on the life-is-how-you-live-it list. That makes 10,569 on mine—or is it 3? Who knows? In any case, I will submit to ME-Bird (but later I must get an accurate count of the one I thought I saw or else enter the taboo mark of an unquantifiable X). I'm thinking the powers that be might not go for my photographic evidence. I would guess they'd whisper "contrived." I really could not care one alula less. The appearance of such an ethereal being stunned me. But I regained my composure, collected my wits, and watched carefully as by thicket dead reckoning and wishful declination, it appeared to be headed north by northwest—guided by the unseen filtered refraction from a waning moon snail shell. Perhaps it is one of those aberrant reverse autumnal migrants. Like me, it chooses to fly against convention, hurling itself headlong into a headwind. Ornithologically backward and by ichthyological salmonid leanings, upstream. Whether taxonomically aligned with shorebirds or the passerine kind, I've got its gestalt down. If it looks like what you think it might be, then maybe it could be not.

The so-called experts who drop names on things might code the shell bird with W-I-T-H. First two and last two letters being recognized convention. But I wanted more. And so without consultation of any authority other than my own, L-O-V-E is the second four-letter code I've assigned. That's the archaic pre-Latinized Anglicized abbreviation for Lesser Opportunistic Vexing Empidonax (some once thought it a flycatcher but have since been proven mostly incorrect—but not quite completely wrong). If you so choose, you can expand and explode convention and call it the WITH LOVE bird. Good? Good. Seems the best way to ID such oddly rare happenstance creatures of memories gone on and future desire is with a singular focus of the heart—and a zoomed-out, close-focused, wide-open mind. Its range is mostly unpredictable, but always check your backyard for molted dreams. That's a sure sign a Wish Thrush has been around. I'm petitioning already for inclusion as a "wistful species." Its status is primarily threatened by a persistent fragmentation of the imagination, demoralizing predation by indoor house cats—and a proliferation of invasive exotic hopelessness.

Joy is the Justice (We Give Ourselves)

Joy is the justice
we give ourselves.
It is Maya's caged bird
sung free past the prison bars,
holding spirits bound—
without due process,
without just cause.

Joy is the steady run stream,
rights sprung up
through moss-soft ground—
water seeping sweet,
equality made clear
from sea
to shining sea,
north to south,
west to east.

Joy is the truth,
crooked lies hammered straight,
whitewashed myths
wiped away.
Stone Mountain
—just stone.
Rushmore
—no more.
Give the eagles
their mountains back.

Joy is the paradise
we can claim
right here,
right now.
No vengeful gods
craving prayer,
no tenth in tithes to pay,
no repenter's cover charge—
no dying required to get in.

Joy is the sunrise
breaking through night's remains,
bright shone new
on a shell-wracked shore;
a fresh tide-scrubbed world
redeems what was,
to is.

Joy is on whimbrel's wings;
the wedge in fast flight,
wandering curlews,
curved-beaks' cries
stitching top of the world
to bottom.

Joy is the soul stirred
underneath the journey,
gaze snagged on wonder,
not knowing final destination,
blessed as a witness,

moored to ground,
worshipful tears
dripped into grateful smile.

Joy is the silent spring,
unquiet.
Rachel's world not come to pass.
The season
dripping ripe full
of wood thrush song.

Joy is all the Black birds,
flocked together,
too many to count,
too many to name,
every one different
from the next,
swirling in singularity
across amber-purpled sky.

Joy is being loved
up close
for who we are.

Joy is the last song,
drifting in
as dark curtains fall;
the sparrow's vesper offering,
whistle lain down
in pine-templed woods,

requiem in me-minor—
church in a cathedral time built.
No stained glass.
No pulpit.
Altars everywhere.
Just listen.
Just look.

Joy is the return,
the wandering warbler
landed in the backyard again,
from who knows where,
to rest,
to uplift lagging spirit.

Joy is the healing,
broken dreams restored—
soaring.
Langston's words
kettling higher
on hopes,
drifting ever upwards
on ragged-mid-lined rhyme,
dancing to syncopated verse.

Joy is our lives mattering,
Blackness respected.
It is seeing my color,
hue not blinded by privilege,

the pious privilege
of claiming you don't.

Joy is the proper name,
with no "n" in the beginning
or "i" or double "g" or "e"
in the middle,
with an "r" rolled hateful
hard at the end.

Joy is your truth
being the same behind my back
as to my face.

Joy is the sharp eye
watching little brown sparrows,
and the kind one,
focused
on little brown children too.

Joy is the ancestors
come before,
surviving the struggle,
staying strong
in the midst of withering storm;
from shackled ancestors
through Jim Crowed back doors
to gerrymandered chokehold now.
Still here in spite of it all.

Joy is the payoff,
for those often down
but never out.
Joy is the thriving,
a people who won't die
in the midst of all this
dying;
the breaths,
ins followed by outs,
easy—
without begging for air
or asking your mama's ghost
to help.

Joy is the drive
with no traffic stops,
with no taillights out,
with no tint technically too dark,
with no speed traps,
with no "yes sir, Officer sir."
No hands at two and ten.
No wondering
where the registration is.

Joy is the flashing blue light
passing by,
not meant for me.
Joy is the good news,
without new dead names,
no chokeholds or murdering knees.

A night of sleep
in your very own bed
without shots in the dark
—no more not waking up,
full of lead.

Joy is the morning jog
without being hunted down.

Joy is the loss
we take to gain,
monuments to traitors
torn down,
lost causes finally buried,
never to be found again.

Joy is the prairie,
where billowed cloud
and wild grass meet;
where the hawks glide
from there to here—
wherever;
its own choice to make,
no border crossing checks.

Joy is the surrender,
to faith of push,
to trust in lift,
giving over to Toni's command
to ride the air.

To float above
the trouble of this world
on a wish.

Joy is my grandma's hands,
grits through gnarled fingers tossed
on cold ground
to snowbirds she pitied—
a love for others
that became my own.

Joy is the wild not tamed,
the rarest beast
with talons sharp,
or long teeth bared,
in the faraway place.

Joy is the wayward weed
in the midtown sidewalk seam,
the one I choose to call
"wildflower"
because it dared
to not be planted,
to not be controlled.

Joy is at the end,
a bruised purpling sky
when the night
comes again,
when luck is metered

by stars winking bright.
Joy is the frogs calling,
amplexus orgying delights.

Joy is the close call
that wasn't close enough.
Death passed by you.
Life stopping by.

Joy is a heart still beating
even though
what could have been—
wasn't.

Joy is the knowing
that what this world
did not give—
it cannot take away.

Joy is the moment
we grab in sweat-soaked
trembling hands,
that slides from possession,
stolen legally in bits and pieces
between yawning cracks
of despair.

Joy is tears,
drops of salt water
fallen in the creases

of an upturned smile.
Joy is the necessity
that must be lain by,
what's kept hoarded in a sturdy cache
ever ready to apply.

Joy is the gift,
just desserts,
what we deserve
without asking
or constant demands—
the comfort that comes
when no one else
really cares.

Joy is the reward,
the salary already earned—
back pay
with four centuries' interest
compounded daily.
At least eighty acres—
and two mules.

Joy is the day off,
just because.

Joy is the kiss of that one,
or the just verdict
delivered by twelve.

Joy is the everything,
the nothing.
The simple,
the complex.

Joy is the silly,
the serious,
the trivial.
The whale enormous,
the shrew's small.

Joy is the murmuration,
then the stillness.
Joy is the inexplicable coincidence.

Joy is what was meant to be.
The mystery of impossibility happening.
The assurance of uncertainty.
Joy is my seeking.
Your being.
It is mine for the taking.
Ours to share.
More than enough to go around,
when it seems nowhere to be found.
Have yourself a heapin' serving.
Have seconds. Or thirds.
'Cause
joy is the justice
we must give ourselves.

Nativist Namaste

ZOOM
Screen
Sometime in 2020

Upon delivering a lecture
to a group of virtual lovers
of all things native, wild, and free,
whose memberships had been faithfully paid
in certain societies,
I was asked at the end of the talk
(emoji applauses duly noted)—
"How will you get your neighbors
to rid their yards of noxious exotic grass?
To eliminate the Bermuda, the centipede
the fescue?
To plant the native things that belong?
Broomsedges, or Paspalums.
You know—bluestems, Indian grass?
Can you convince them to go native?"
My answer, past a barely suppressed eye roll
and the heavy sigh that I only half-hoped
they could not hear past mute
or catch in the glare of the too bright
ring lamp bouncing off my
receding hairline
was in my head:
I really don't know how much
my neighbors will care

about native warm season grasses
or wildflowers locally raised
and pollinator safe,
when their health is threatened by viral strain
or heightened likelihood of being fatally police
detained
or worrying over the job that's gone—
I cannot in good faith ask them
to nuke with poison
the green they now have,
to ask people who might have hungry stomachs,
emptying wallets,
maybe emptying lungs—
to destroy the little they have
to satisfy some vision
of perfect piedmont prairie
that once was cherished lawn.
All of this swirled round in pre-verbal
thought response.
Then—I opened my mouth
"No," I replied, firmly out loud.
"I don't think I will—I haven't tried."
The virtual crowd sat quiet.
I glimpsed a head shake
or maybe it was just an "s-m-h" vibe I got.
No yellow hands clapping showed up
in the little people-filled boxes.
My lack of eco-conversion conviction

of restoration awareness
was not so appreciated.
Just a few days later, another chance.
This time about the birds (not plants)
and what is, and is not
properly wild.
Then too,
the host wanted to know
what might my thoughts be on
why skin color matters sometimes,
more than Empidonax flycatcher identity.
Having given my Black birder opinion on
offenses taken personally
over the prosecution and profiling
of dark-skinned humans
(and black feathered things—like calling
double-crested cormorants "nigger geese"
or blaming Negroes for quail disappearing),
It was time for Q&A.
Hands went up.
I took them as they came,
gave easy funny quips about being stuck
on butcher birds (i.e. loggerhead shrikes),
offered advice on where best to see
Swainson's warblers.
Then a chat question rolled up—
"But what can I do about the house sparrows?
They are pushing my poor bluebirds out!"
The questioner seemed desperate in all caps.

Apoplectic at having the Eurasian weaver finches
anywhere around.
In remote solitude I smiled wryly—
swallowed hard, gritted my teeth through
the screen, then replied—
"Not so sure house sparrows
are your biggest problem, ma'am.
Sure, they may usurp (yes I used the word)
a nest or two
of what some would deem 'more desirable kinds'"—
(then inwardly began mid-sentence,
a thought process—a conversation
wholly within about the Nazi scientist's love affair
with what belonged and what didn't.
Wasn't there some idea of master types
of this and that floating about?
How did that scheme of exclusion and homogeneity
turn out?)
—but
I kept that train of thought
on its own internal track with only me on board—
and hitched for a second on revealing a musing
of racial purity politics and its proximity to nativist ecology
but instead, I said aloud,
"The cats roaming your neighborhood
are the worse players in this bird's
declining-by-billions tragedy.
Keep them inside and your bluebirds will
be better off.

Don't blame beings
who never asked to be here
for their presence
but found a way to thrive
in spite of fickle minds
who'd just as soon destroy
them once their service is done."
I proceeded to mention starlings,
the beauty of murmurations viewed from afar,
the hate of the same birds up close,
tears of joy to words of hate—
the way we accept some for who they are
then deny others life because of the same—
depending on how close to us they come
or how far away they stay.
The room went quiet.
From the Zoom squares
where these questions grew
through a thicket of oblivion and blind spots
a touch screen of shattering silence.
Kind of like the one
from the old bird club guy,
a white man who advised behind a half smile
that I "get over" racism
because he resolved the Holocaust
by practicing Tai Chi.
Six million plus exterminated—
but martial arts in a park made it all better
for him.

My constant reminding
that things weren't so good for too many
birds and Black folks alike was too much.
He declared
(with the same shitty smile),
"Get it together and you'll feel better.
Be more positive! It's not all that bad."
He waved.
I did not wave back.

I looked into his square—
Wondered if George Floyd ever thought
in his last moments
that downward facing dog would save his life.
I did what that Black man,
face full of asphalt,
was denied by a knee on his neck,
and breathed deep as I could
with a long slow blink,
to keep anger and tears back.
"*Namaste Motherfucker,*"
was what wanted to pour out,
but all I could do in that moment
was think of how this idiot
was the problem with so much.
"Next question, please,"
dribbled from between my lips.
The Tai Chi birder, the Holocaust happy birder

sat confident in his prescription
as I struck second-thoughts from my repertoire.
Made speaking first mind
requisite condition.

Yard Wild Robin

run-stopping, run-stopping, cocked head downward looking—
in my backyard.
Wondering as it short-slip-thrush glides through the green pseudo-prairie of annual rye
now gone human calf high,
if from somewhere close by
—or distantly faraway—
she's come to be here.

Perhaps from some near treeline northerly up-there place where worms are frozen—or distastefully frigid at best. Do the grubs in the warm clay of my southern Piedmont taste better than those in any other yard? Why here, Dear Robin?
Is there a better chance of escaping the coop's quick talons in my privet hedge
gone wild?
Of course, I must blame the waxwings in part for its presence. They seem hell bent on eat-shatting it out on a regular basis. I know, I'm too tolerant of such things.
Wondering though,
does the rusty chain link at least give you a fighting flight's chance at escaping the long- haired orange tabby from across the street who fancies my half acre his hunting jungle?
Or is it by chance that you are here in this moment? All brick red-breasted and slate-rock gray backed run-stopping,
run-stopping in the chill rain damp?
Does everyone really know who you are?

So common that so many ignore

your ubiquitous charm?

Just so you know, I heard a story of a bird that like you was once numerous beyond counting—or care. It filled the skies with millions of its kind for days and broke branches from large oaks in which it rested.

So common that everyone certainly had to know its name. Men killed it because they could. "Too many to count,"

that's what they said as they kept shooting.

I didn't ask you your preference, by the way. Should I continue to call you "Robin"? Would you rather "*turdus*" or maybe "*migratorious*"?

Oh yeah, before I forget—that bird I'm speaking of that streamed like coming night against the midday sun has gone away now. Disappeared.

The last was named Martha. Died in a cage. Alone. I shudder, thinking as I watch you run-stopping head-cocking that there'll be more to come.

So, what might I call you? Did you ever say? Is Robin good enough?

My grandmother called you by first and last name, "Robin Redbreast."

She loved seeing you. My brother not so much. He once ate one of your kind, grilled on a spit after aiming too true with his BB gun.

For that I apologize.

So should I wait until your rarity makes you worthy of notice?

Nothing like death to make us look behind to see if the sins we've committed are catching up.

Robin it is then. Come back soon, okay?

I'll leave the grass mostly uncut and let the privet grow.

I'll keep throwing four-letter-not-so-nice words that begin with "f" and end with "you" at the tabby.

—just for you, Robin.

Winter Kill

The cold comes hard here,
drops sudden,
           falls heavy.
Borne far above the lake-locked land
it descends to
render the rivers
           still as though they never ran.
Clouds the mirrored waters
        beneath
slick glazed shield that sends the loons crying
south—
later now than in the old days, when
Gichi-gami went thick,
When *Baashkaakodin Giizis*
wished it so.
Yet—it comes.
      The cold comes to make soft ground solid
 shrinks autumn waning light
   to dim
then draws the doors shut on days
so that only the dull slivers shine through.
        The cold sends the sun to wait on solstice.
   The cold comes to make living hard.
The cold is not quaint or subtle.
   It gives no quarter. There is no comfort
in the cold, save deep slumber
or dying.
Winter cold is a lynx that chases warm fleeing
to other seasons—

or else to flounder as hapless prey in chilled jaws.
But, I cannot speak of your cold
beyond dreaming.
I only know of it when ravens let rumors
fly loose
on somnambulant winds blown on dreams.
Awk! Awk! Awk!
They circle and soar to tell me of winter,
where snow is stubborn. Where ice hides time.
Where cold is master of every being.
The raven calls me between rapid eye blinks to see the
  wild things huddled against the cold,
or secreted away in dank burrow or worm-worn hole.
Oook oook oook oook ooook!
The raven insists I dream, see one wild thing set upon the other
wild thing
 to sate hunger
   or starve.
Wild things know the cold. Live in it.
  Die by it.
Gaagaakshiinh, the raven who remains in my dreams
 past the others flown into nothing
—tells me
that the cold is not cruel to his band of black kindred,
but kind because the hooved ones
will provide.
That there is no planning
the two-toed kind make,
(she claims) when the hunger calls.

When the river pack howls
 darkness
            down
        to drape the great woods
                        in moonlit shrouds.
and in fear,
says *Gaagaakshiinh*.
The moose's withers tremble like slender twigs,
as he rises long-legged from piss warm bed.
Long ears swivel to catch the dog's chorus,
The deer stir in their yards,
stare doe-eyed into gray shadows thrown
    on lunar lit drifts to catch glimpses of the end.
 By sun's next rising white lain down before dawn,
        will lie stained red,
the black ones count;
Ook ook
Oook oook oook
Raven math divines one less to browse spring tender shoots
one less to secret fawns in fern soft woods
    for the black bears
                to reclaim half.
One less to suckle life by summer's long mosquito-thick days.
One sacrifice to feed all who will come after the pack fills bellies
to swollen.
It is the way of things
when winter comes.
The cold is a blade.
The wolves are blades made
to thin the herd.

The raven tells me of it in these dreams,
and I listen because she is wise in ways that I am not.
For I do not know of your cold, or wolves or moose.
I do not know of terror to the bare bone
the deer know when death is sure.
Gaagaakshiinh claims (with great-beaked authority)
     that the cold will take
what the wolves cannot catch
That those left standing will cleave stronger
  to the land come warmth of warm moons.
A time coming absent the slow, absent the careless.
In my raven-fed winter dreams, I am told
that the great gray owl witnessed this necessary thinning.
The cold blade honing the pack's cunning.
Taking by tooth and claw life once burning hot
now cooling
      spilled out.
The owl (says *Gaagaakshiinh*)
sat on the edge of it.
Sat still on a tamarack's bent bough.
Slow blinking in the flakes head turning from one day to the next.
It sat as the snow fell,
each flake
      falling as if each would become mouse.
The owl watched the waifs slip through spruce—
at first, the crackling
of icy crust giving
        beneath each step,
Raven counts a pair, then another
and another. There, one more.

I saw in my dreams through the owl's eyes
        by way of the raven's mouth
the pack circling the meadow clearing,
                each wild dog's breathing fog
exerted to same strategy.
Chase. Kill. Eat.
Hot canid breath rose to clouds of death to come.
        One by
one,
single-filed plans made,
            chase designed
each threads silent
                as snarling pike under still lake glides.
  A shoulder
            then ribs
urgent haunches tensed.
Never all at once, only bits of the whole.
  A glimpse of hide—
yellow eyes glow.
        Knowing that it is better to be seen afar
            than be smelled close in fear.
They enter mortal stage downwind. Final act begins.
The woods, darker than black
            fills with deer bolting riot.
        The herd slogs in nightmare
    wrapped in black raven seeing. Black man dreaming.
And the great gray owl saw firsthand,
        as told by the raven
                (who know everything of cold but sat huddled warm
together in the darkness)

Heard every lung-labored gasp,
    brown shadows scattered.
Saw when the beasts of the long night made short another hooved life.
The muffled snarls. Flesh tearing. Eyes walling
Last gasps of ruminant memory drained.
    Whitetail becomes wolf in gulps.
The snow fell. The cold gnawed at the fat marrow.
All slid into silence.
Dead Quiet.
    Whiskey jacks came noisy at first light.
The raven floated in at dawn.
She called black band in to glean,
krook!krook!krook!
        chickadees chatter to draw lots for shreds
left between bones.
An eyeball left staring glazed into blue sky is *Gaagaakshiinh* prize.
Ermine hid where it stood, waiting a turn.
The drifts grew deep as snow falls once more.
The owl saw, told Raven,
    who told me.
I woke into a void full of sharpness, silence, fear death,
but empty of all that had been. All that was.
and then—
I shivered. Knew your cold.
As Raven told it to me.

On Edge

Crepuscular—
dawn and dusk.
The hours on edge.
Moments
to shine
in shadow;
to celebrate the possibility
of shifting shapes
attached to something else.
A time to wax reclusive;
reunion with the introvert,
to bond by hoot,
reconnoiter by howl.
Find comfort where most
do not.

Nine New Revelations for the Black Bird-Watcher

Revelation #1
Hooded warblers are lucky. They can wear hoodies and no one asks questions or feels threatened. Vigilante 'Mericans don't mobilize to make citizen's arrests if they loiter in a strange shrub for too long.

Revelation #2
No one denies the eye-bending beauty of a painted bunting by saying, "I don't see color."

Revelation #3
Roadrunners don't get gunned down for jogging through neighborhoods, do they?

Revelation #4
Why are some immigrants accepted and others not? Asking for a European starling.

Revelation #5
Double-crested cormorants are insulted at still being known as "nigger geese" by some. Can they at least get "Negro" as a less hateful nickname?

Revelation #6
Why do people cry and set music to far-away murmurations— the swirling, whirling, wheeling aerial ballets of flocking birds—but then hate the very same birds up close? Asking for the same European starlings from #4 and lots of befuddled blackbirds.

Revelation #7

Wondering if some white people tell crows and ravens how impressed they are with their articulate intelligence, as if blackness precludes the confluence? Wondering if the corvids tire of it. I do.

Revelation #8

Has there ever been a white bird as hated as a black or brown one?

Revelation #9

Birds don't mind if we misidentify them, 'cause they know who they are without our labels. What they truly despise is the disrespect of habitat destruction, pollution, hordes of free-roaming outdoor cats, and the catalog of stupid things humans do to make their already difficult lives harder.

Breathe

Breathe in now
deeply as you can,
pull every molecule of this life
into your being,
every bit of love and goodness
you ever had the pleasure of giving
or the gift of receiving.
Suck it into your marrow bone,
do not let it stop at your lungs.
Hold on…
Now
that it is all in
              release it out—
to be a free bird in flight.
Exhale this next existence,
liberated as if it were everything
—and your last thing,
because it may be.
Now,
breathe in again,
                 now out. Again.
Repeat
until you cannot.
Thank all the good gods you know
in between
chest rising,
chest falling
for your blessed still-living lot.

Dam

A thing standing strong,
grown tall,
beside a thing built by hands,
a creation of need—dry hay.
Some place to forestall rust. To rest the mules.
A thing someone planned.
A thing someone measured twice,
maybe cut once. Cursed when a thumb
intercepted a hammer meant for a nail.
Hoping for square. Trying for level.
Wondering if the joints would hold
Now falling in. Work by time undone.

Not a mile west, sits another thing
standing strong—
built of things once standing
now lain low by persistent gnawing.
Sticks, mud, rotting leaves, mats of weeds—
built stout by paws, a certain calculus;
rule of flat tail and claw,
plans passed down by creek,

before a thing wanting out.

The question of failure creeps in.
Which thing fails first?
The one built of hands and saws
or by tooth and claw?

Hammer & Saw or Pen & Pad?

I can't paint well without numbers or sculpt more than soap or carve wood without bleeding or dance without tripping or sing outside the shower—so there are days I must hammer and nail and saw to beat lumber into submission; to maul and coerce boards into cooperating until the lot of them become something usable and not an eyesore for someone to condemn. Once done tagging dimensional scraps together, when my thumbs have been mis-aimed, hit, and mashed into bruised pulp and sweat-drained to pillars of salt, I write, body sore and spent, possibly bruised, but mind and heart freed to create because a certain kind of dues have been paid.

River Unnamed

I need to know
what the Cusabo called
the big wide ribbon of
semi-salty water,
the fat stretch of river
that snakes between
salt marsh and the high
ground with the Pink House
I claim by rent in December
February
April and May.
That stretch of my so-called
Paradise sitting on land
stolen to become Bleak House.
What did the Edisto
say to the Esamacu,
or the Stono, to know the
highs or lows by full moon
or crescent?
Did all the people before
white ones came,
Combahee, Wimbee
Kiawah, Etiwan
Wambo,
call the strong run
of deep wet by a special name?

Do the dolphin stranding
mud minnows on oyster bank know
by squeaks or squeals or other
identifying label?
Perhaps it is the way
the kingfisher rattles,
the eagle whistle-cackles,
the thin rail clappers.

"Townsend River,"
seems the easy white way out.
Besides,
I choose not to baptize my
hopes in the names of those
who might see me more as mule to trade
than man to respect.

Slack Tide

Tide slacks
between decisions
high or low,
argues with itself
to stand still.
The arc of the tides:
rails win,
bald eagle's cackling cry
gets close second
for first bird.
Sun easts, tide pushes out,
rises to oblique overhead,
heaven bound.
sky slides to red-edged blue.
Sun wests, river runs in.
Then dark to night,
moon big as a china plate rises,
clapper rails approve,
no standing applause
required.

More Salt Marsh

I am more marsh side still
than surf's roll or murmured sound.
I am summer tired,
dull green as late August spartina,
waiting on autumn's October polish
to burnish my rods to gold.
I remember spring as not-so-long-ago rebirth,
by resurrection of
my new sun-grown verdance.
I am painted bunting's
artful plumage spill
on a myrtle bush.
Nest secure in Spanish moss.
I am more clapper rail
than sanderling.
Chase was never my thing.
I have always been
a slip through the shadows
kind of bird;
more cryptic brown mystery
than see-me-bright right now.
I am more pluff mud
than sugar sand.
Reputation by aroma
sometimes precedes me.
More sulfur-scented soil sensual;
more rut musk stink than sweet.
More buck deer on a rub line
no one else can see.

More muck than dune.
More river otter than dolphin.
More loggerhead shrike
than turtle.
I am sometimes no place anyone desires,
beyond hermit crabs and whimbrels.
I am slower creek
than fast flow;
more tidal surges than sea level rise.
Call me black skimmer.
I am wrack left behind,
splined to winding,
to define momentary past tense.
I am more sunset than sunrise
—some days—
until the reverse becomes true.
Because new conflagration on the east horizon
renders preference for one beauty over
the other,
moot.
It is foolish anyway
to choose awe over joy.
I am edge of the wet, where dry begins.
Where uphill finds downstream.
I am thicket tangled rank on hammock
high ground,
where diamondback rattler reigns.
I am all that converges in wanting.
I am at soul's wild heart,
marsh side.

Some Advice

If you can,
find some corner of the world
at peace.
A sliver of green. Water serene.
Wherever nearby. Far away.
Go there. Burrow in. Listen to birds.
Talk with frogs.
Turn off what you can't control.
Turn on to something wild.
Be bold in your silence.
Do what you can where you are
to notice,
to nurture something good.
Something kind.
Something that slows your heart
quiets the mind
to drip-trickled thoughts—
even as the world shouts.
Let many desires rise
to a single love.
Whisper a prayer on the wind
to North, East, South, West
to whatever god(s) you wish.
You do not have to bow
or kneel.
Go straight on the winding path
at him or her or them.
Climb if you must. Sit.

Rest. Be still
Ask for better.
Demand it.
Then—
breathe.

Joy, As It Comes

More than twenty blackbirds murmurating in an orange evening sky
Any sparrow singing from a weed top
Sunrise
Sunset
Full moons with names
Birds without hateful people's names
Autumn at its blushed orgasmic peak
A sounder of baby pigs escaped from whatever pen once held them
Acceptance of a butterfly lit on my hand to suck sweat salt from my skin
A whiskey buzz good enough to loosen the conversation just a bit
Finding the precocious trillium in March braving late frost
First frost on fern fronds
A salamander red as fire in a cool spring pool
A tug of unknown origin on the end of a wet fishing line
A clear EKG
A whitetail buck believing himself unseen
First ovenbird in the April woods
"TEACHERTEACHERTEACHER!"
The voices of thrushes migrating in nighttime skies
Woodcock in an old field wet swale being called to heaven by lust

Wild Goldfish

Today,
they are not pet store-bought
quarter-a-piece carelessly dipped
from a too crowded tank
throw-aways,
for tossing to
some toothy captive oddity,
named Oscar.
Today,
they are not trash carp
to be disposed of
when floating belly up
swirled down to county sewer hell
by toilet bowl rapture
or suffocated slowly
in tiny cheap bowls
won at a county fair.
Today,
they are wild furtive fishes of the
Kidney Pond Shaped Sea
(which is fed by the Greater Hose River
which feeds over Found Stone Falls
over and over again)
hiding behind shadows
darting between ripples
as would headwater trout
as would salmon going out to
return to the same stream.

Be Wild!

Seek wildness. Wherever. However. Find the freedom of the tether torn away from tame, whether it be worshipping a single bird flying or a galaxy of stars light-stitched in darkest sky, calling you to get high on endless time. Find wildness. Treasure it. Roll in it and stink of it. Claw, scratch, and scuffle to remain in it. Raise nose to the wind and travel towards its seduction. Stay close by and conjure it to you. Burrow down into it. Climb high to reach it. Sleep in it. Sleep with it. Go feral first if you must. Escape. No, self-liberate, instead. Break out. Run, slither, gambol, slide. Jump over. Jump up. Rub head on cedar trees to tatter-mark where your heart has claimed it all. Piss on pawed-up ground. Squat behind bushes. Grunt! Bellow! Scream! Grow! Dance the crane two-step! Howl! Migrate over watery gulfs to fall out in it the next morning. Ride the tides and breach blow. Catch squirming bliss in your mouth and swallow it whole. Swim upstream to spawn in it and know that in your last acts, reality rotting away but still somehow knowing, the final spurt of joy lain in the riffle will bear more.

Pine Warbler

What
must the pine warbler
on the other side
of the window glass
think
as time passes on my side
in ticks and tocks?
A life
metered out by schedules
deadlines. Calendars,
clocks.
Expectations.
Disappointments.
They all add up.

But how
does a bird measure
beyond season?
Or sunrise and sunset?
Maybe they count
dawn songs, nests, eggs,
mates, close calls with hawks
narrow escapes from cats
or windows not met in death.

Maybe it is stars bright enough
to direct travel at night as we sleep,
waiting on alarms
to tell us when we've had enough.

Perhaps it is some accounting
for journeys between
this place and that.
A calculus of landscapes spanned.
Rivers crossed.

Whatever
meter winds in the tiny sprite's mind,
cannot be known
by mine.

And so,
as the hours pass
I find I less need to know anything
except how to find
more time
to watch a bird
be a bird.
No watch on either of our wrists
required.

My Space

I crave the wide open wild; the span of those places where I can see earth meet sky, where restless seaside melds by surf and surge into saltmarsh; ragged brackish edges ruled by moon, measured by tide. I am Black skimmer then, dragging soul's bill to catch what I can. I am drawn to rolling prairie under waves of nodding grass. There, free to graze with my big wooly head bowed to ferruginous hawk gods who bless curlew's long bill and cud chewer's wanderlust with broadly spread wings. Tundra quilt spread sub-arctic wide beneath Denali shadow seems as much home, as home, somehow. I am hump-shouldered grizzly then. Content with whatever I might gather or hunt, at peace alone. But not lonely.

If I must climb, then I'd rather fly. I will be raven then, a black being on constant watch. In a pinch, even piedmont pastures dotted with cattle draw my heart out; a reminder too, of home place. The furrowed brown of plowed soil or the briar guarded margins of overgrown old fields, the domains of harriers and shy sparrows, are second-nature haunts.

In the close-by spaces where wild is hemmed in by hard packed ground, I will say, "Oh, give me land, lots of land under the starry skies above, don't fence me in!" That song could be my anthem.

So then why have I created such small spaces with walls in which to be? Why would a large person, seek a ten by sixteen side yard cabin-like writing shack filled beyond full of bits and pieces of my life. A thicket of books, papers, carvings, talismans, paintings, sketches, scribbled notes in scraps of paper, rocks, feathers, and empty box turtle shells. Secrets I won't reveal.

And the other, a tiny home on the edge of the Blue Wall:

Sunset Camp. It is my other small space tucked away in the corner of a dark corner. It's eight by fourteen, just big enough for my six-foot-three-inch, broadly girthed body, to stretch out inside. There's less room within for a complete archiving of my life. Art from a few friends hangs. There are some books. Bourbon. I rest easy within but must exit to change my mind.

It is a curious juxtaposition, the horizontal expanses I demand. The cramped claustrophobic interiors I create.

What dissonance within my psyche requires both?

A seer friend saw it simply. Explained it with one small word: "den." These are your dens, she said. You were a bear, maybe wolf in a past life. This is where you go to feel safe.

It made sense to me instantly. I look in the mirror, and there staring back is a broad, brown face harboring small ursine eyes. I shuffle in a pigeon-toed way when I walk. More bear waddle than human stroll. I treasure the company of a select few at select times. Peaceably irascible, I'm a live-and-let-live until poked or provoked kind. Outside, I need as much open ground as can be found. Inside the shelters I've burrow-built, comfort is essential. Walls that embrace with a lover's familiarity.

I must be able to come and go, on a whim. To go into deep slumber when the season or sentiment calls. Some call it the blues. For us bear folk, it's the browns.

I want my cave and to wander wildly beyond it, too. It is my greedy bear nature to bend to spatial desire in this way. To forage widely with random intimate purpose. Inner me. Outer me. I desire every bit of wild water, air, and earth that I can traverse. The sum rolled into one, ursine man.

Gifts

Wondering today on the gift of an orange-crowned warbler looking into my Thicket window and feasting on suet. A near arctic-breeding, winter-visiting warbler, wing to wing in my yard, with lemon-yellow pine and butter-butted, yellow-rumped cousins. I'm happiest to provide for them and the other birds. Obsessing today, though, on the orange-crowned. What are the chances that this little olive-drab beauty could be the same green sprite I held in my hand in Denali after it perceived window glass to be open subalpine tundra sky and by sickening soft thud collision, came to rest as if dead, on my cabin porch? One in a billion? A less than lightning striking in the same bottle while winning the super Powerball riding a rainbow-colored unicorn probability? Would some complex calculation of orange-crowned population size adjusted by survival rate and likelihood estimation factor of range size give a sensible answer?

Or maybe it's just a one in the wisher's heart's chance of thinking that this world is smaller by the years advancing and by the birds stitching hemisphere to hemisphere. My place down here, patchworked to their place up there. It is smaller too, by the kindness shown by so many of you—kindred spirits and friends and well-wishers showing up in my social media window today, my birthday. It has been an overwhelming joy, like the wild birds that I watch, to read each one. Each greeting has been a gift I hold close to heart like the little orange-crowned that lay still in my palm that day, then blinked once, twice, to sit up full of life and fly off into the scrub to maybe find nest or mate and make more of itself. What are the chances that this little orange-crowned warbler that looked in my South Carolina window is that same Denali bird, delivering some gift of its presence? Slim and none, the statisticians would say. Improbable at best, they would caution. Next to none, would be the rational mind's choice. But I'll let the bean counters and naysayer modelers have their numbers, for now. I'm claiming highly unlikely today, as my sure-bet desire. My gift of wonder given to me. I'm afflicted with this whole idea of birds and endless possibilities. That foolishness bleeds over sometimes into people too.

Ten Rules for Going Feral

1. Never walk a straight line. Those routes are the institutionalized ones leading to not so good ends. Voltage charged chairs, rooms with forever sleeping beds from which you'll never arise. Instead follow the flowing irregularities nature draws—the ever-changing splines of surf or shell wrack left by high tide. Track the fox's four-toed wander along a pond's muddy margin. Trail the doe's cloven hopscotch to get nowhere faster than browsing heart's-a-bustin' will allow. Learn from the swallow and take dips and dives as privileged flight.

2. Wake before the dawn chorus and sing your own song of sunrise.

3. Follow a whippoorwill's wailing to the dark holler where it calls loneliness and feel its wanting as your own.

4. Stray away from drama. Let wildness find peace in you.

5. Tell secrets to birds (or butterflies or boulders or bullfrogs or bats) and know they will go no further than the next bird (or butterfly or boulder or bullfrog or bat).

6. Shun concrete. Shutter convention.

7. Feel earth somewhere on your bare human flesh; between toes or fingers on face or whatever you dare to expose.

8. Be willing to become deer or mouse or thrush or wasp or wildflower. Be fish. Be newt. Be belly low and see the undersides of mushrooms.

9. Curiosity must never wane but make allowances for ignorant bliss.

10. Stay away from rules that make you otherwise than who your heart tells you to be.

Wrens

The wrens
are in full force this morning
relentless in their wrennishness
babbling in fern tangles, probing the pitcher plants
summiting the woodpile, searching under hosta leaves
scaling the knee-high pile of stacked stones—as if
they could not care less, be more unconcerned
with politics, polls, breaking news,
broken promises, choices removed, doom coming
by next election or give one
holy tinker's damn
about all I worry on.
How dare they
live their
lives being
free of
me.

Moldered

Memory is leaves
                    falls
tumbling
senescence reveals true bearing
        bared
to empty limb,
having given green over to mapling scarlet.
        Hickory turns gold. It is all flash.
all flurry—
the end of life for uncountable fading lot;
    oak to brown
curls
crisps to death.
                    One
  of uncountable millions done when
wind comes to reap life away.
        All present soon passes
    moldered
  to   cold   ground
          slow back to soil
where all begins,
        again.
Heart sleeps warm beneath the rot
    remembers what leaves
forget.
Until sun reminds.
Spring comes.

Coffee Black

I do not feel
      particularly-hyphenated
today.
No, I'll take my identity straight;
      no chaser.
No sugar, no cream.
No African. No American. No Miscegenation.
Just Black—
with a capital "B".
  A hot brimming colored cup
of what you see.
What used to be your Negro,
now coarsely ground me.

Retreat!

Comes the order
in the face of withering fire,
bugle blaring, flag upside down
waved frantically.
Panic is close at hand.
Retreat!
Comes the command
to turn tail and run
backs against the wall
to flee what would otherwise do us in.
Fighting is no longer priority.
Retreat!
The realization that fortune is fucked,
that survival has fallen
to improbable,
victory unlikely
against insurmountable odds.
Retreat!
The only choice left
as tactical troubles surround to lay siege
with an up shit's creek snowball's chance in hell
chance at anything good happening.
Retreat!
The desperate call of the meeting maker
when the gathering
will go for longer than it should.

Retreat!
Is the wild wanderer's choice,
for some sheltered refuge, off grid
beyond being easily found,
away from swamp-mucked
four-walled responsibility.
The place where no attack
is required, no offense need be taken
except to find self, getting lost.

Fifteen Rules for Better Being

1. No meetings without a clear agenda, unless with birds or wild beasts or those tending toward such.
2. The "transaction" must benefit me. Mutual good should be a common denominator. Make symbiosis sacrosanct.
3. Don't try to make sense where there is none to be made.
4. There is no work "emergency" unless you've signed on for such. Don't respond to work requests during your time. No one will ever value the minutes remaining in your life like you do.
5. Don't seek those who don't seek you. Surround yourself with those who have your best intentions in mind, all others keep at arm's length or dismiss to other realms of relationship.
6. Treat time alone as a gift. (*See* 5)
7. Clearly define what it is someone would have you do. If the work is beyond your capacity of will or want, politely decline without hesitation. Avoid those who make habits of patronizing leg pissing to make it feel like a warm spring rain. In the end, it will turn cold and stink for all.
8. Set your own expectations. Move the bar if necessary and without guilt.
9. Redefine "productivity" daily. Some days, "productive" means a new poem, a new bird, or maybe one breath following the next.
10. Make the word "no" a comfort word. It will become more palatable with use as it is an acquired taste.
11. Make "sphere of my control" a mantra. All else chill, hope, pray, curse…whatever gets me through.
12. Shun fame. Do not seek fortune. When either finds me, be thankful, try to leverage for good and move on to what's next.

13. Moderate… except for when sheer bliss is guaranteed.

14. Limit assumptions. Take a beat. Think before you speak. Take a beat. Then think again.

15. A response is not always necessary. Don't play catch when the ball is being thrown AT you. Only play when it's being thrown TO you.

All That We Carry (forever incomplete)

for Nikky Finney who carries so much for us in her words

All that we carry

in gourds grown strong
along rivers we cannot remember

in wooden Senufo bowls on a mama's head

in memories of sons who never returned
in prayers

in goatskin bags
in our seasick middle passaged bellies
wretched out in the dark below

in memories of sons who never returned

in burlap sacks dragged down long cotton rows
in jugs of Edgefield clay
name scribed in stoneware,
rules to not read or write ignored for the sake
of freeing self

in willow creels full of mullet fish
head on not split

in sweetgrass baskets from marsh at low tide
winnowing rice in the breeze

in cast nets thrown from clenched snaggled teeth
wrigglin' shrimp full in prayers

in leather satchels with notes to pass
from this plantation to that

in raggedy bundles tied to hard hickory hoe handles
when Harriet came up the Combahee

in tin tubs full of jubilee neck bones
in cast iron pots too heavy to move
in wrapped up quilts
patched together from precious scraps
in pokes, in grips migrating to Detroit or maybe DC
in second-hand suitcases to Fisk or Talladega
in greasy brown paper bags
taken from side windows way 'round back

in open caskets that should not be

in memories of sons who never returned

in prayers to gods who don't listen

in lunch pails to the March
in purses refusing to sit in the back
in pockets turned inside out on illegal search

in skulls no longer fondled for what they called science
carrying ideas to make a nation rich

in wounded hearts asked again and again to be the better person
with knees on our necks

in laptop satchels carrying uneven redlined chances
in bank accounts with pennies on the white dollar
in dreams interrupted by death being Black

in memories of sons who never returned

in prayers
despite all this,
we carry you, America
still
clinging to our backs

in prayers
for our mothers
for our fathers
for our sons
for our daughters
for others

we remember,
all we carry

Gratitude

Grateful for wild birds and a heart that leads me to write about, for, and to them. Thankful to all who read these words and love the birds, as I do.

Thankful to the ancestors whose blood, sweat, and tears have nourished fertile ground for me to share creative passion. My success is a direct effect of their struggles. I stand on the shoulders of their strength and persistence.

I'm deeply appreciative of family (not always blood) and friends (not always seen) who support close-in and far away the convergent work of art and science that I do. That they *see* me and this meandering path as worthy, means life itself.

To the publishers, editors, fellow writers, poets, and kindred spirits who read, review, mark up, revise, put up with and otherwise, give heart, head, and printed space to on pages, and bind it up into books. You have helped me leverage the great gift of free expression that gives voice to my passion.

Thank you to every human being who has opened a door to my wild leanings, from earliest barefoot country boy days on dirt roads, to ivory tower climbing, to present day eclectic rambling. You provide a guiding star to the sparrow, whom I envy. Your attention to my work in print and social media feed is like rising warm air to the swallow-tailed kite, with whom my spirit soars. It is fluted thrush song in spring wood. It is the shrike's way that impales me deeply so that I'm stuck fast on wildness, as a means for reconciling my place as part and parcel, not anything else.

It is my hope that in this effort of *Joy* bringing, a few lines blur on the continuum of time, space, and identity to bring us all closer together.

Amen.

Glossary

Autumn
When the sun, by equatorial (permissible) kisses, tempts leaves to blush and birds (here) to fly south.

Black
An anti-matter hue to way too many. *See also* Black Whole.

Crow
A large corvid "guilty" of being black and smart. *See also* Raven and Paul Robeson.

Denali
Tallest peak in Alaska that sees everything, even when you can't see her. Formerly misnamed after a rotund president no one remembers as mountain-naming worthy.

Dolphin
Small marine and brackish (semi-salty) water whales with teeth for eating fish. Highly intelligent and social, they may be the reanimated spirits of enslaved Africans self-liberated by jumping into the Atlantic, or else thrown overboard because of perceived worthlessness as property. *See also* Merperson.

Entropy
The tendency for everything to droop, drop, drip, or disappear; body parts included.

Fall

What autumn does when the wind undresses it.

Feral

A state of lessened domesticity trending towards wild. My preferred status dynamo.

Georgia O'Keeffe

Brilliant artist with a penchant for making flowers seem sensual beyond their botanic Eros. A bloom-in the-eye-of-the-beholder kind of being.

Heart

The muscular organ lubdubbing blood and passion to other parts of the body. Also a passion pump.

Hummingbird

Smallest feathered things with jet engines for hearts and helicopter rotors for wings. Fueled by nectar, sugar, and jealousy.

If

Two letter word upon which everything depends.

Joy

Blessed assurance that wild birds (or butterflies, or beasts, or unfettered breathing) will continue to be, in spite of what has been, is, or is yet to come.

Kill

To take life, or that which gives it.

Lunar

Moon-y. Howl-worthy heavenly body. Lust Orb.

Love

To give of one's most sacred life essence to some other person, place, or non-human being.

Marsh

A muddy mucky grass-growing water-ruled rail heaven.

Nature

Everything around us not built. Everything inside us not bought.

Nurture

To care for, protect. To provide for. To hold close with intent on wishing the best beyond self.

Out

Opposite of in (or within), and freer too, to just be.

Pine Warbler

A stay-at-home winter warbler, lemony yellow to drab gray as February sky. Named for where it's found and not after some fallible human being.

Question

Everything.

Rules
Standards and regulations to guide one's behavior, applicable to most (except for Supreme Court Justices).

Reparation
Repair following recognition of a wrong and reconciliation of that wrong to what should be. A monetary debt unlikely to ever be paid. It can be joy taken without asking or permission. Ancestral claim as a human being to happiness despite attempts to suppress otherwise.

See
To view or look upon. Or, if so soulfully inclined, to imagine beyond. No sight required. Insight and vision highly recommended.

Slack Tide
The moments of still water. A resting indecision between high and low.

Thrush
Robin-sized birds varying from moss-backed olive brown to fawn shaded; shy forest dwellers with dappled shadow breasts; to more sociable cobalt and electric blue birds, with rusty chests. Yes, robins, with gray feathers and brick red fronts, swamp-lovers now converted suburbanites, are included. *See* Yard Hopper.

Ursine
Bearlike. Waddling, shuffling, making do with what comes, asking mostly not to be fucked with. Prone to long naps and

intense eating. Intensely loyal to wild home. *See* Grizbro-Dougie Peacock.

Vexed

To worry, as in why there are no words that begin with the letter "v", to place in one's pithy glossary. *See also* "Y" and "Z".

Wild

Free to roam untethered and unquestioned, with no time to be home. *See* Unplugged.

Xenophobia

Sin of mass hate; nativists bent on restoring an intolerant "great again" state.

Yearning

For more time in places where wild birds outnumber human faces; a county in the State of Want, located somewhere between Lowcountry South Carolina saltmarsh and Blue Wall Holler, Montana prairie, Vermont verdance, Alaskan sub alpine tundra and southern Piedmont home. *See also* Paradise, also Heaven-on-earth.

Zero

Tolerance for haters. The one intolerance allowed. But *see also* Willful Ignorance.

Zora Neale Hurston

Proudly unapologetically southern Black woman who went North to find freedom to write her life story, but never let her heart wander far from the woods and wetlands she loved back home. She wandered as she wished and loved as she dared. A woman way ahead of her time, and most other folks, Black or white, couldn't take her being her. *See also* Hero, Role Model, Writing with Authentic Urgency.

J. Drew Lanham is the author of *Sparrow Envy: Field Guide to Birds and Lesser Beasts* and *The Home Place: Memoirs of a Colored Man's Love Affair with Nature*. He has received a MacArthur "Genius" Grant, the Dan W. Lufkin Conservation Award from the National Audubon Society, the Rosa Parks and Grace Lee Boggs Outstanding Service Award from the North American Association for Environmental Education, and the E. O. Wilson Award for Outstanding Science in Biodiversity Conservation from the Center for Biological Diversity. He served as the Poet Laureate of Edgefield, South Carolina in 2022. He is a bird watcher, poet, and Distinguished Professor of Wildlife Ecology and Master Teacher at Clemson University. He lives in Seneca, South Carolina.

 **HUB CITY PRESS** | PUBLISHING
New & Extraordinary
VOICES FROM THE
AMERICAN SOUTH

FOUNDED IN Spartanburg, South Carolina in 1995, Hub City Press has emerged as the South's premier independent literary press. Hub City is interested in books with a strong sense of place and is committed to finding and spotlighting extraordinary new and unsung writers from the American South. Our curated list champions diverse authors and books that don't fit into the commercial or academic publishing landscape.

RECENT HUB CITY PRESS POETRY

The Last Saturday in America • Ray McManus

El Rey of Gold Teeth • Reyes Ramirez

In the Hands of the River • Lucien Darjeun Meadows

Thresh & Hold • Marlanda Dekine

Reparations Now! • Ashley M. Jones

HUB CITY PRESS gratefully acknowledges support from the National Endowment for the Arts, the Amazon Literary Partnership, the South Carolina Arts Commission, the Poetry Foundation, and the Chapman Cultural Center.